# How to Play Funny Fill-In!

Love to create amazing stories? Good, because this one stars YOU. Get ready to laugh with all your friends—you can play with as many people as you want! Make sure to keep this book on your shelf. You'll want to read it again and again!

## Are You Ready to Laugh?

- One person picks a story—you can start at the beginning, the middle, or the end of the book.

- Ask a friend to call out a word that the space asks for—noun, verb, or something else—and write it in the blank space. If there's more than one player, ask the next person to say a word. Extra points for creativity!

- When all the spaces are filled in, you have your very own Funny Fill-In. Read it out loud for a laugh.

- Want to play by yourself? Just fold over the page and use the cardboard insert at the back as a writing pad. Fill in the blank parts of speech list, and copy your answers into the story.

Make sure you check out the amazing **Fun Facts** that appear on every page!

2

To play the game, you'll need to know how to form sentences. This list with examples of the parts of speech and other terms will help you get started:

**Noun:** The name of a person, place, thing, or idea
Examples: tree, mouth, creature
*The **ocean** is full of colorful **fish**.*

**Adjective:** A word that describes a noun or pronoun
Examples: green, lazy, friendly
*My **silly** dog won't stop laughing!*

**Verb:** An action word. In the present tense, a verb often ends in –s or –ing. If the space asks for past tense, changing the vowel or adding a –d or –ed to the end usually will set the sentence in the past.
Examples: swim, hide, plays, running (present tense); biked, rode, jumped (past tense)
*The giraffe **skips** across the savanna.*
*The flower **opened** after the rain.*

**Adverb:** A word that describes a verb and usually ends in –ly
Examples: quickly, lazily, soundlessly
*Kelley **greedily** ate all the carrots.*

**Plural:** More than one
Examples: mice, telephones, wrenches
*Why are all the **doors** closing?*

**Silly Word or Exclamation:** A funny sound, a made-up word, a word you think is totally weird, or a noise someone or something might make
Examples: Ouch! No way! Foozleduzzle! Yikes!
*"**Darn!**" shouted Jim. "These cupcakes are sour!"*

**Specific Words:** There are many more ways to make your story hilarious. When asked for something like a number, animal, or body part, write in something you think is especially funny.

adjective

famous person

year you were born

noun, plural

something gross

body part, plural

animal

something creepy, plural

liquid

type of dinosaur

adjective

exclamation

adverb ending in –ly

another body part

animal sound

food

verb ending in –ing

something fast

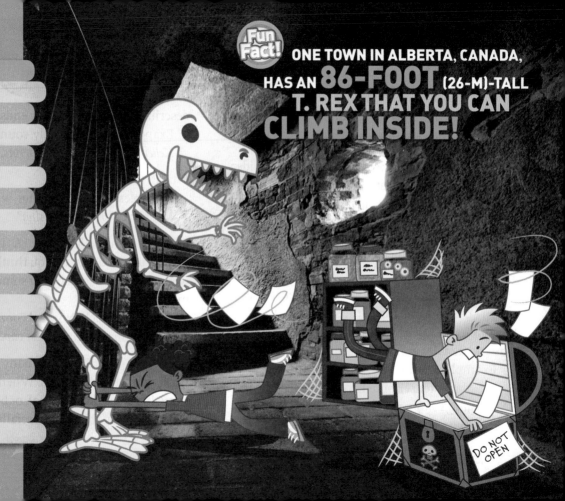

ONE TOWN IN ALBERTA, CANADA, HAS AN **86-FOOT** (26-M)-TALL T. REX THAT YOU CAN **CLIMB INSIDE!**

DO NOT OPEN

**A Scary Start**

There it is, towering above me on this _____ night: the _____ Museum
                                          adjective                            famous person

of Natural History. It's been closed since _____ . People whisper that _____
                                              year you were born                        noun, plural

haunt it. But I've finally worked up the courage to go inside. So I slip into the basement through a half-open,

_____ -covered window. Slowly, my _____ adjust to the dark, and I
   something gross                                body part, plural

can see what's in the shadows: a(n) _____ skull, jars full of _____
                                        animal                              something creepy, plural

floating in _____ , a life-size model of a(n) _____ . Next to me sits a large
              liquid                                        type of dinosaur

_____ trunk with " _____ !" painted on its lid. _____ , I pry it open
   adjective              exclamation                        adverb ending in -ly

and stick my _____ inside. I can't see anything, but I hear a faint " _____ !" It also
              another body part                                                  animal sound

smells like _____ . I lean in a little more. Suddenly, I'm sucked inside and _____
              food                                                                        verb ending in –ing

through the air at what feels like the speed of a(n) _____ —in total darkness.
                                                      something fast

- adjective
  - body part, plural
- large number
  - fruit, plural
- something huge
  - verb
- animal
  - noun, plural
- verb
  - another body part, plural
- adjective
  - color
- something gross
  - noun
- verb
  - something stinky
- verb
  - noun, plural
- adjective

**Fun Fact!** DINO POOP FOSSILS ARE CALLED COPROLITES. THE **BIGGEST ONE** EVER FOUND WAS **17 INCHES** (43 CM) LONG AND **7 INCHES** (18 CM) WIDE!

The first thing I notice is a thud. It's getting _____ (adjective) and louder. I open my _____ (body part, plural)—

no wonder I couldn't see anything—and then I see it: a(n) _____ (large number) -foot-tall *Tyrannosaurus rex*. Its teeth

are as big as _____ (fruit, plural) , its claws the size of _____ (something huge) . And it's coming

straight at me! I _____ (verb) to my feet and run like a(n) _____ (animal) toward a heap of

_____ (noun, plural) . As the T. rex closes in, the ground begins to _____ (verb) violently, and I'm

knocked to my _____ (another body part, plural) . _____ (adjective) , I look for a new place to take cover. I see

it, my only shot: a big, _____ (color) pile of dino _____ (something gross) . I hold my _____ (noun) and

_____ (verb) in. The scent of _____ (something stinky) is overwhelming. I _____ (verb) around

inside as the dino's _____ (noun, plural) draw nearer. They pause near my hiding place, and then pass.

I burst out and take a(n) _____ (adjective) breath. I've gotten away. But not clean.

something gross

    noun

type of breakfast food, plural

    favorite food, plural

something sticky

    insect, plural

adjective

    noun

verb

    color

adjective

    number

type of job

    body part

verb

    noun, plural

noun, plural

    animal, plural

another body part

Fun Fact! MOST DINOSAURS COULD SWIM.

Prehistoric Pool Dip

Hiding in dino _____ saved my _____ , but now I'm a mess. My skin is smeared
                    *something gross*                    *noun*

with half-eaten _____ and rotten _____ . My ears are clogged
                *type of breakfast food, plural*                *favorite food, plural*

with warm _____ . And my hair is crawling with tiny, wriggling _____ .
          *something sticky*                                                    *insect, plural*

I decide I've got to get _____ , and quick. I clean out my ears and hear the sound of a(n)
                        *adjective*

_____ in the distance. So I _____ toward it, and soon I see a bright _____
      *noun*                              *verb*                                              *color*

waterfall cascading into a(n) _____ lake _____ feet (m) below. I'm an expert
                            *adjective*              *number*

_____ , so I dive _____ -first into the lake. The moment I splash through its surface,
      *type of job*              *body part*

I feel better. I _____ beneath the waterfall and let it scrub the _____ and _____
                  *verb*                                                          *noun, plural*          *noun, plural*

off me. Tiny _____ gobble them up while swimming circles around me. Finally clean,
            *animal, plural*

I float on my _____ and start to wonder how I wound up in this prehistoric place.
              *another body part*

- adjective
  - noun
- dance move
  - noun, plural
- noun, plural
  - prehistoric animal, plural
- noun, plural
  - shape
- something tall, plural
  - verb
- number
  - past-tense verb
- body part
  - noun
- verb
  - silly sound
- verb
  - verb ending in –ing
- cartoon character

Fun Fact!

SCIENTISTS HAVE UNCOVERED MORE THAN 2,000 SABER-TOOTHED CAT FOSSILS FROM TAR PITS IN CALIFORNIA, U.S.A.

**Sticky Situation**

I decide I've got to explore this _____ world more. So I slip out of the _____ and
                                    *adjective*                                        *noun*

_____ into a forest of _____ and _____ . I hear the chatter of
*dance move*                      *noun, plural*       *noun, plural*

_____ and the whir of _____ overhead. In the distance, I see
*prehistoric animal, plural*        *noun, plural*

a(n) _____ dinosaur head poking above _____ . I'm looking up, up, up when
      *shape*                                      *something tall, plural*

suddenly I start to _____ down, down, down. I'm already _____ inches (cm) deep when I realize
                     *verb*                                        *number*

what's happened: I _____ into a tar pit! Quickly, I wrap my _____ around
                    *past-tense verb*                                  *body part*

a(n) _____ at the edge of the pit. But it breaks loose and tumbles into the tar with me. Next, I grab
      *noun*

a vine and _____ hard. With a(n) "_____!" I break free from the tar, only to
             *verb*                          *silly sound*

have the vine _____ and send me straight back in. I'm _____ downward
               *verb*                                            *verb ending in –ing*

when I hear a voice that sounds like _____ say: "Let me help you."
                                      *cartoon character*

type of dinosaur

friend's name

adjective ending in –er

something gross

verb

food, plural

something gross, plural

size

verb

number

your age

noun

animal

body part, plural

utensil, plural

adjective

something slippery, plural

large number

**Fun Fact!** *TYRANNOSAURUS REX* COULD GULP DOWN SOME SMALL DINOSAURS WITHOUT EVEN CHEWING

**Dining With Dinos**

Having dinner with dinosaurs is a really *big* deal. I'm at the home of the _____ that
_____ (type of dinosaur)

rescued me from the tar pit. Her name is _____ . She's much _____
_____ (friend's name) _____ (adjective ending in –er)

than the T. rex who chased me into a pile of _____ . I try not to think about that as I
_____ (something gross)

_____ my dinner: a heaping portion of barbecued _____ with a side of steamed
(verb) _____ (food, plural)

_____ . I take _____ bites, and _____ in between them at
(something gross, plural) (size) (verb)

her and her family. She has _____ brothers and _____ sisters. So it's a pretty big _____
(number) (your age) (noun)

we're seated at. To reach it, I'm sitting atop their pet _____ . I eat with my _____
(animal) (body part, plural)

because the _____ the dinos use are too big for me. My host warns me not to fill up—
(utensil, plural)

she caught _____ _____ for dessert. Turns out it's a special occasion:
(adjective) (something slippery, plural)

Her youngest sister is turning _____ today.
(large number)

exclamation

relative's name

type of dinosaur

favorite singer

favorite song

body part, plural

verb ending in –ing

adjective

another song

electronic gadget

name beginning with "D"

adjective

noun, plural

verb

instrument, plural

verb ending in –ing

holiday song

language

noun

HAPPY HATCHDAY

Fun Fact!

*CORYTHOSAURUS* COULD LIKELY **BLAST TRUMPET SOUNDS** THROUGH ITS BONY, CURVED CREST TO COMMUNICATE WITH ITS HERD.

# Dinosaur Karaoke Hatchday Party

After dessert, my dinosaur friends invite me to their sister's karaoke birthday party. I can't believe my luck.

"_____ !" I say, and we head out to their friend _____ 's house. When we
　　exclamation　　　　　　　　　　　　　　　　　　　　relative's name

arrive, the party's already in full swing. A(n) _____ with a voice like _____
　　　　　　　　　　　　　　　　　　　　　type of dinosaur　　　　　　　　　　　　favorite singer

is onstage singing "_____ ." The crowd is going wild, raising their _____
　　　　　　　　　　favorite song　　　　　　　　　　　　　　　　　　　　body part, plural

in the air and _____ to the music. I'm so _____ , I sign up right away to
　　　　　　verb ending in –ing　　　　　　　　　　　adjective

sing "_____ ." When it's finally my turn, I grab the _____ from
　　　　another song　　　　　　　　　　　　　　　　　　　electronic gadget

DJ _____ and start belting out the lyrics on the screen: "_____
　name beginning with "D"　　　　　　　　　　　　　　　　　　　　adjective

_____ _____ !" My dino friends grab _____ and join me
　noun, plural　　　　verb　　　　　　　　　　　　　instrument, plural

onstage, and soon we're all _____ in harmony. Afterward, we sing "_____ ."
　　　　　　　　　　verb ending in –ing　　　　　　　　　　　　holiday song

in _____ to their sister, and the whole room wishes her a happy _____ .
　language　　　　　　　　　　　　　　　　　　　　　　　noun

time

number

verb ending in –ing

type of dinosaur

clothing item

body part

verb

noun, plural

hometown

emotion

sound ending in –ing

insect, plural

something big, plural

verb

adjective

command

direction

verb

**Fun Fact!** THE BIGGEST **FLYING REPTILE** WAS *QUETZALCOATLUS*, WHICH HAD A **40-FOOT** (12-M) WINGSPAN.

After a crazy dinosaur party, I notice it's already _____ —we must have spent _____
                                                        time                                              number

hours _____ ! A flying _____ offers me a ride back to the home
       verb ending in -ing              type of dinosaur

of my dinosaur friends, so I grab its _____ and hop onto its _____ .
                                            clothing item                              body part

We _____ over the _____ and soon I can see the whole dino town below me.
      verb                          noun, plural

It reminds me of _____ . I get a little _____ and think again about
                      hometown                              emotion

how and when I'll get back to my home. Suddenly, I hear a loud _____ sound, and
                                                                       sound ending in -ing

before I know it we're surrounded by a swarm of _____ . Only they're huge, the size of
                                                      insect, plural

_____ ! I hold on tight as we _____ through them, their _____
  something big, plural                        verb                                 adjective

wings just missing me. "_____ _____ !" I yell at my ride. But just then a wing
                              command              direction

whacks me in the face, and I _____ off the dinosaur and into the air.
                                   verb

- noun
  - body part, plural
- verb ending in –ing
  - adjective
- noun, plural
  - verb ending in –ing
- noun
  - another body part, plural
- adverb ending in –ly
  - adjective
- something fuzzy, plural
  - adjective
- farm animal
  - musical instrument
- food
  - number
- verb
  - noun

**Fun Fact!** T. REX'S VISION WAS BETTER THAN THAT OF A HAWK.

# Lost in the Dark

I've landed in a(n) _____ (noun). I wiggle my _____ (body part, plural) to make sure nothing's broken after my fall off a(n) _____ (verb ending in –ing) dinosaur. Everything seems _____ (adjective). So I shake the _____ (noun, plural) off me and start _____ (verb ending in –ing) back to my friend's house. But I'm lost. And it's totally dark—I just tripped over a(n) _____ (noun). So I'll have to use my _____ (another body part, plural) to feel my way out of here. And listen _____ (adverb ending in –ly). I'm moving along through what feels like a thick pile of _____ (adjective) _____ (something fuzzy, plural) when I hear a(n) _____ (adjective) noise. It sounds like a cross between a(n) _____ (farm animal) and a(n) _____ (musical instrument). Whatever's making it is close. In a few seconds, I smell its _____ (food)-like breath—it's only _____ (number) inches (cm) away now! I _____ (verb) in fear and decide it might be safer to just stay put until the _____ (noun) comes up. But I'll sleep with one eye open!

something soft, plural

past-tense verb

adjective

large number

your age

noun

color

type of pattern, plural

verb ending in –s

adjective

noun

verb ending in –ing

verb

your favorite dinosaur

verb

exclamation

verb ending in –s

silly word

adjective

**Fun Fact!**

THE **LARGEST** DINOSAUR EGG COULD HOLD ABOUT AS MUCH FLUID AS **85 LARGE** CHICKEN EGGS.

**Baby Dinosaur**

When I wake up in the morning, I finally see where I've spent the night: in a nest made of _____ .
<small>something soft, plural</small>

No wonder I _____ so well last night. It's a(n) _____ nest—it takes me
<small>past-tense verb</small> <small>adjective</small>

_____ steps to walk across it. And in the middle of it are _____ eggs. I try to guess
<small>large number</small> <small>your age</small>

what type of _____ will hatch from them based on their appearance: _____
<small>noun</small> <small>color</small>

_____ . But I can't think of anything that _____ like that. All of a sudden,
<small>type of pattern, plural</small> <small>verb ending in –s</small>

a crack forms in one of the eggs. A(n) _____ _____ pokes through and begins
<small>adjective</small> <small>noun</small>

_____ . I wonder if I should _____ it. But just then the egg splits open and
<small>verb ending in –ing</small> <small>verb</small>

reveals a(n) _____ ! We _____ at each other.
<small>your favorite dinosaur</small> <small>verb</small>

I say, "_____ !" It _____ and says "_____ !"
<small>exclamation</small> <small>verb ending in –s</small> <small>silly word</small>

This is so _____ ! I wonder where its mom is.
<small>adjective</small>

- verb ending in –ing
- adjective
- noun
- color
- large number
- emotion
- adverb ending in –ly
- body part
- something gross, plural
- animal noise
- another body part, plural
- something slimy
- verb
- something wet
- adjective
- noun
- exclamation
- verb

**Fun Fact!** MOTHER *MAIASAURA* BROUGHT FOOD TO THEIR BABIES AND COVERED THEIR NESTS WITH LEAVES.

**Don't Mess With Mama!**

The shaking is faint at first. I don't even notice it. But soon I have trouble _____ (verb ending in –ing), and the

_____ (adjective) nest I've fallen into is shaking. I cling to its _____ (noun) and then see what's

coming toward me: a mama dinosaur. She's bright _____ (color) and _____ (large number) times the size of her

baby that I just saw hatch. And she seems _____ (emotion) to see me. _____ (adverb ending in –ly), I crawl to

the top of the nest and throw my _____ (body part) over its side. Then I stop short. The nest is surrounded

by _____ (something gross, plural)! " _____ (animal noise)!" I hear behind me—the mama dino is hot on my

_____ (another body part, plural). So I grab a(n) _____ (something slimy) and _____ (verb) myself out of the

nest toward _____ (something wet). Mama dino is so close now I can feel her _____ (adjective) _____ (noun)

on the back of my neck. " _____ (exclamation)!" I shout, and _____ (verb) as fast as I can.

type of liquid

temperature

noun

type of dinosaur

verb ending in –ing

verb

type of pet, plural

noun

prehistoric animal, plural

gymnastic move ending in –ing

favorite song

color

clothing item, plural

adjective

verb

relative's name

friend's name

verb ending in –ing

**SEA TURTLES** GREW TO
**12 FEET**
**(4 M) WIDE**
**DURING THE DINOSAUR ERA!**

Fun Fact!

I'm lucky—I make it to the _____ lake just in time to hide. I plunge into it—it's a pleasant
                                    type of liquid

_____—hold my _____, and wait. I need to make sure the _____
temperature                      noun                                              type of dinosaur

that was _____ me is gone. When it seems safe, I _____ to the surface, take a
          verb ending in –ing                                    verb

deep breath, then go back under for a look around. I swim past a school of _____ and
                                                                             type of pet, plural

into a giant _____. There, I see two _____ _____
              noun                                 prehistoric animal, plural   gymnastic move ending in –ing

in sync to "_____." They're wearing matching sparkly, _____
             favorite song                                          color

_____, and their movements are _____—they seem to be
clothing item, plural                         adjective

experts at this. I _____ over to them and introduce myself. Their names are _____
                    verb                                                                   relative's name

and _____. And, it turns out, they're _____ for the Dinosaur Olympics—
     friend's name                                   verb ending in –ing

which are happening tomorrow!

 **Fun Fact!**

BASED ON TRACKS, THE **FASTEST DINOSAURS** WENT ABOUT **26 MILES AN HOUR** (42 KPH).

- emotion
- planet
- large number
- something big
- verb ending in –ing
- noun
- type of dinosaur, plural
- body part, plural
- noun, plural
- small number
- noun
- type of job
- superhero
- verb
- verb
- favorite snack, plural
- famous athlete
- last song you heard
- verb

I am super _____ to be at the Dinosaur Olympics. It's like the Olympics on _____ —only
                  emotion                                                                planet

_____ times bigger! I take my seat in the _____ where the games are being held and
  large number                                        something big

wave to the synchronized _____ dino duo I met yesterday. They won a(n) _____ earlier
                          verb ending in –ing                                      noun

for their routine. Up next is the smash-off event, in which _____ compete to see who can use
                                                            type of dinosaur, plural

their _____ to smash the most _____ in _____ seconds. They make
      body part, plural               noun, plural       small number

a(n) _____ , and after it's cleaned up, the *Tyrannosaurus rex* take their places for the arm-wrestling
     noun

competition. When the _____ yells "_____ !" the dinos clasp hands and _____
                      type of job           superhero                                        verb

back and forth. They growl and _____ and bare their teeth. Finally, a winner is announced, and the
                               verb

crowd begins to chant "_____ !" At the closing ceremony, _____ sings
                       favorite snack, plural                         famous athlete

"_____ " backward, and I'm very impressed. We all stand and _____ .
 last song you heard                                                      verb

- adjective
  - silly word
- verb ending in –ing
  - type of dinosaur
- body part
  - dance move
- noun, plural
  - shape
- your name
  - another type of dinosaur, plural
- verb
  - verb ending in –ing
- another body part
  - year you were born
- verb
  - verb
- verb ending in –ing
  - noun

**Fun Fact!** *TRICERATOPS* TOES POINTED **OUTWARD.**

# Dino Dance Party

When you're dancing with dinosaurs, you have to be very _____ (adjective). One misstep, and _____ (silly word)!

So to be safe, I'm _____ (verb ending in –ing) tiptoe on a(n) _____ (type of dinosaur)'s _____ (body part) while

we do the _____ (dance move). We're pretty good _____ (noun, plural), it turns out. Soon others

form a(n) _____ (shape) around us and start chanting: "Go, _____ (your name)!" I see that a group

of _____ (another type of dinosaur, plural) nearby is also drawing a crowd. They're pretending to _____ (verb)—

the latest dance craze. And in the middle of the dance floor, a few dinos are watching a *Triceratops* show off

by _____ (verb ending in –ing) on one _____ (another body part). Then the DJ puts on the _____ (year you were born) hit

"Everybody _____ (verb) the Dinosaur," and every last dino in the room starts to _____ (verb).

Suddenly, I'm in a sea of stomping feet and _____ (verb ending in –ing) tails. It's not long before one

whacks me off my dance partner—and right out the _____ (noun).

noun, plural

verb

letter

color

pattern

verb

body part

adjective

large number

vegetable, plural

clothing item

something sticky

adjective

fruit

verb

exclamation

your age

type of dinosaur

sports equipment

**Fun Fact!**

THE FIRST FORESTS—
WITH TREES, FERNS, AND HORSETAILS—
GREW IN THE
DEVONIAN ERA.

# Unpleasant Prehistoric Plants

I stand up and brush the _____ (noun, plural) off me. I've been thrown out of a dino dance party. But I'm OK

with it. It was time to _____ (verb) anyway. So I set off down a(n) _____ (letter)-shaped trail that winds

through a forest full of strange plants. There are clumps of _____ (color) _____ (pattern) flowers that

_____ (verb), and when I lean in for a sniff, they bite my _____ (body part). _____ (adjective)

vines hanging from _____ (large number)-foot-tall _____ (vegetable, plural) try to wind their way into my

_____ (clothing item) as I walk past. And I have to make sure to steer clear of puddles of _____ (something sticky)

that ooze from _____ (adjective) trees. Toward the end of the trail, a carnivorous _____ (fruit) snaps at me,

and I _____ (verb) into one of the puddles. Stuck in the muck, I shout out, "_____ (exclamation)!"

Luckily, a(n) _____ (your age)-year-old _____ (type of dinosaur) from a nearby

school hears my cries and comes to my rescue with a(n) _____ (sports equipment).

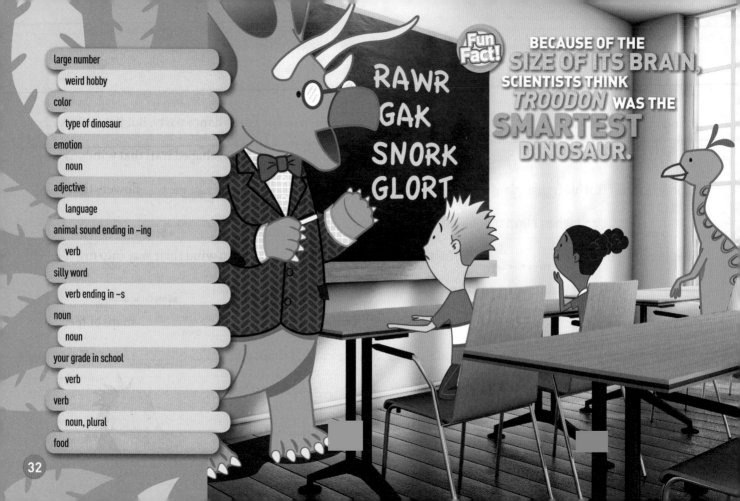

- large number
  - weird hobby
- color
  - type of dinosaur
- emotion
  - noun
- adjective
  - language
- animal sound ending in –ing
  - verb
- silly word
  - verb ending in –s
- noun
  - noun
- your grade in school
  - verb
- verb
  - noun, plural
- food

RAWR
GAK
SNORK
GLORT

Fun Fact!

BECAUSE OF THE SIZE OF ITS BRAIN, SCIENTISTS THINK *TROODON* WAS THE SMARTEST DINOSAUR.

It's my first day at dinosaur school and already I'm in trouble. My new dino friend and I are _____
_____ minutes late to _____ class, and the teacher, a(n) _____ -haired _____

*large number*  ·  *weird hobby*  ·  *color*  ·  *type of dinosaur*

is _____ . I find an empty _____ to sit in and try to follow along. But I'm totally

*emotion*  ·  *noun*

_____ . The lecture is in Dinosaurese, which sounds like a combination of _____

*adjective*  ·  *language*

and _____ . So I'm relieved when class is finally over and we all _____ outside

*animal sound ending in –ing*  ·  *verb*

for recess. The dino kids invite me to play _____ , a game in which everyone _____ to

*silly word*  ·  *verb ending in –s*

see who can create the biggest _____ that breaks a(n) _____ . I try it, and to my surprise,

*noun*  ·  *noun*

come in _____ place. Afterward, I suggest we play _____ and go _____ .

*your grade in school*  ·  *verb*  ·  *verb*

While a *Stegosaurus* counts, I run deeper into the _____ to find

*noun, plural*

a good _____ . Soon I'm so far in, I don't know where I am!

*food*

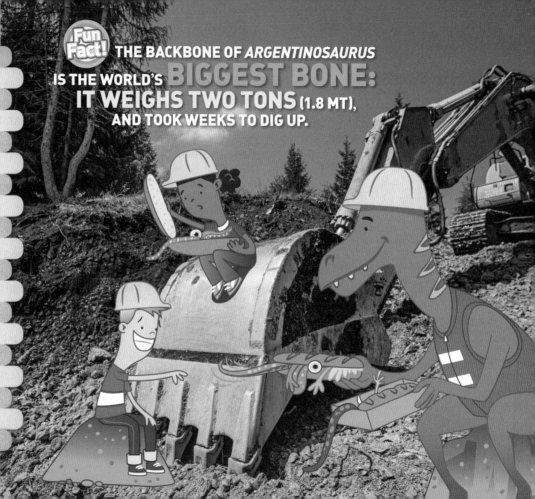

fun place

    shape

large number

    adjective ending in –est

type of dinosaur

    type of machine

something heavy, plural

    another type of dinosaur, plural

tool

    verb

noun

    something enormous

command

    clothing item

something hard, plural

    adjective

emotion

    celebrity

something gross

**Fun Fact!** THE BACKBONE OF *ARGENTINOSAURUS* IS THE WORLD'S **BIGGEST BONE: IT WEIGHS TWO TONS** (1.8 MT), **AND TOOK WEEKS TO DIG UP.**

# Under Construction

I'm lost in _____ (fun place) —again! But I think I've found a way out: by following a set of _____ (shape)

-shaped, _____ (large number) -toed footprints. I'm hoping they'll lead me to my friends. But instead, after a few

miles (km), they lead me to the _____ (adjective ending in -est) place ever: a dinosaur construction site! It's a giant

pit, and at its edge a(n) _____ (type of dinosaur) operating an XXL _____ (type of machine) is lowering a load of

_____ (something heavy, plural) to the bottom. There, a crew of _____ (another type of dinosaur, plural) is using a huge

_____ (tool) to _____ (verb) a(n) _____ (noun) . I can tell they're building a(n) _____ (something enormous) .

A dino who spots me shouts, "_____ (command) ! Put this on!" and tosses me a(n) _____ (clothing item) .

They're all wearing one, so I slip it on. They put me to work blasting apart _____ (something hard, plural) .

It's a(n) _____ (adjective) job, so I'm _____ (emotion) when I hear _____ (celebrity) announce

it's lunchtime. Until I learn that lunch is _____ (something gross) sandwiches.

- large number
  - noun
- room in a house
  - something squishy
- electronic gadget
  - your favorite TV show
- type of dinosaur
  - actor or actress
- verb
  - verb
- type of insect, plural
  - type of appliance
- sport
  - verb ending in –ing
- another type of dinosaur, plural
  - adjective
- emotion
  - animal noise
- body part

**SCIENTISTS HAVE NOT BEEN ABLE TO BRING DINOSAURS BACK TO LIFE LIKE IN JURASSIC PARK**

Fun Fact!

SNAX

**What's on Dino TV?**

I'm really excited to watch dinosaur TV. My friend's TV is huge—_____ feet (m) across! And as the
                                                                    *large number*

_____ of honor, I get the best seat in the _____, a(n) _____, and
*noun*                                          *room in a house*   *something squishy*

control of the _____. I turn on the TV and am delighted to find my favorite show,
               *electronic gadget*

_____—only it stars a(n) _____ instead of _____!
*your favorite TV show*          *type of dinosaur*         *actor or actress*

We settle in and don't _____ until the episode's over—we're totally into it. Then we take a quick
                        *verb*

break to _____ and grab a bag of _____ from the _____
          *verb*                        *type of insect, plural*    *type of appliance*

to snack on. Afterward, we watch a little dino _____ before getting sucked into a show about
                                                *sport*

fearsome, _____ _____. It's super _____, and we
          *verb ending in –ing*  *another type of dinosaur, plural*   *adjective*

agree we're _____ it's not real. Just then, we hear a loud "_____!"
            *emotion*                                              *animal noise*

and a T. rex _____ smashes through the wall—for *real!*
             *body part*

POP CORN

37

- adjective
  - noun
- type of dinosaur
  - exclamation
- verb
  - verb ending in –ing
- clothing item
  - body part
- type of furniture
  - verb
- adjective
  - adjective ending in –est
- noun
  - verb ending in –ing
- adjective
  - another body part
- small number

**Fun Fact!** *ANKYLOSAURUS* HAD AN **ARMORED BODY.** EVEN ITS **EYELIDS** WERE **COVERED IN ARMOR!**

The first few seconds of getting caught in a dinosaur battle are _____ . I need a(n) _____
                                                                    adjective                                    noun

to realize that a T. rex and a(n) _____ are fighting—right on top of me! "_____!"
                                   type of dinosaur                                        exclamation

I yell, to get their attention. But they can't _____ me over all the _____ .
                                                verb                              verb ending in –ing

When the T. rex's tail knocks my _____ off my _____ , I decide to take cover.
                                  clothing item             body part

I flip over a(n) _____ and _____ behind it. Then I realize how _____
                 type of furniture      verb                                      adjective

that is. So I decide to head for the _____ _____ . But before I can reach it,
                                      adjective ending in –est    noun

a giant dino foot blocks my path. Without _____ , I hop on and cling to its _____
                                           verb ending in –ing                         adjective

skin. I figure it's better to be on a dino than under it! It's a wild ride and soon I've slipped to the tip of its

_____ and see the ground is only _____ inches (cm) away!
another body part                          small number

- verb ending in –ing
  - something soft, plural
- large number
  - verb ending in –ing
- adverb ending in –ly
  - body part
- adjective
  - noun
- size
  - animal
- type of clothing
  - emotion
- something tiny, plural
  - verb
- adjective
  - silly word
- another body part
  - verb

Fun Fact!

**A SEQUENCE OF PRESERVED DINOSAUR FOOTPRINTS IS CALLED A TRACKWAY.**

# In a Dinosaur's Footsteps

I've been stepped on, but not squished by, a dinosaur, thanks to it _____ in a pile of
    verb ending in –ing

_____ . I count myself lucky, until I look up and see I'm _____ feet (m) deep
something soft, plural                                                    large number

in its footprint. And then I notice something _____—there's something alive in here!
                                                verb ending in –ing

_____ , I poke it with my _____ and feel a(n) _____ _____ .
adverb ending in –ly              body part              adjective            noun

A(n) _____ _____ wriggles out and starts gnawing on my _____—it's
       size          animal                                                type of clothing

trying to eat me! _____ , I step back and pick up a handful of _____ to
                   emotion                                                something tiny, plural

_____ at it. Soon more of the _____ creatures wriggle their way out of the
    verb                                adjective

footprint, and I'm surrounded. "_____!" I say, to try to communicate with them. Suddenly, a
                                 silly word

superlong _____ drops into the footprint—something from above is offering me help.
          another body part

I grab it, and _____ up and away, to where I don't know.
                verb

least favorite class in school

shape

adjective

body part

number

another body part, plural

language

your age + 1,000

silly word

something gross

adjective

noun, plural

adjective

type of insect

vegetable, plural

verb

liquid

adjective

size

Fun Fact! THE WORD "DINOSAUR" IS DERIVED FROM GREEK AND MEANS "FEARFULLY GREAT LIZARD."

I think twice about my escape from _____ once I see what's rescued me. It's a
_____least favorite class in school_____

dinosaur—I think. Its head is _____-shaped, and its arms are unusually _____ .
_____shape_____                                          _____adjective_____

And though it appears to be missing a(n) _____ , it has _____ extra
_____body part_____                                 _____number_____

_____ . As strange as it looks, it speaks _____ , so we're able to introduce
_____another body part, plural_____                    _____language_____

ourselves. It's a _____-year-old _____-saurus named _____ .
_____your age + 1,000_____    _____silly word_____              _____something gross_____

It seems _____ enough, so I agree to have dinner at its house. Once there, I see its _____
_____adjective_____                                                       _____noun, plural_____

are _____-looking too. Over a meal of _____-stuffed _____ ,
_____adjective_____                          _____type of insect_____        _____vegetable, plural_____

I work up the nerve to ask why they _____ the way they do. "We like to experiment," my host
_____verb_____

says, and hands me a cup of hot, bubbling _____ . I want to be _____ , so I take
_____liquid_____                                 _____adjective_____

a(n) _____ sip. And then I start to feel funny.
_____size_____

- body part
  - small number
- another body part
  - large number
- planet
  - verb ending in –ing
- verb
  - room in a house
- verb
  - adjective
- faraway place
  - adjective
- liquid
  - something big, plural
- noun
  - animal
- superhero

**Fun Fact!** HUMANS DIDN'T APPEAR UNTIL 62 MILLION YEARS AFTER DINOSAURS WENT EXTINCT.

## Dino for a Day

In the blink of an eye, my _____ (body part) triples in size. In _____ (small number) seconds, my

_____ (another body part) grows _____ (large number) times bigger. And by the time I say, "What on

_____ (planet) is _____ (verb ending in –ing)?" I've grown so much that I can't _____ (verb) at the table

anymore. It's crushed beneath me as I burst through the _____ (room in a house). I feel myself _____ (verb)

until I'm so _____ (adjective) I can see all the way to _____ (faraway place). When I look down, I get

a(n) _____ (adjective) surprise: I've turned into a dinosaur! Those weird dinos I was dining with must

have fed me magic _____ (liquid). I lift my new legs and am amazed at how thick and heavy they are—

like _____ (something big, plural)! Then I swing my tail—and accidentally take out a(n) _____ (noun).

Oops! When I open my mouth to speak, a roar as fearsome as a(n) _____ (animal)'s comes out instead—

awesome! I feel like _____ (superhero)!

adjective

noun, plural

type of flying object, plural

type of dinosaur, plural

command

body part

large number

something lightweight, plural

noun

another body part

your name

something soft, plural

noun

animal

verb

adverb ending in –ly

hometown

type of furniture

emotion

MANY DINOSAURS HAD **SPIKES** ON THEIR BACKS AND TAILS.

Fun Fact!

I'm starting to think I make an awesome dinosaur—but the others disagree. I'm not used to my new,

_____ body, and I've already smashed a dozen _____. A fleet of _____
    adjective                                        noun, plural                    type of flying object, plural

flown by _____ surrounds me and orders me to _____. I swat
         type of dinosaur, plural                              command

at them with my _____, and they open fire, pelting me with _____
                body part                                                large number

_____. I laugh—until I realize I'm turning back into a(n) _____.
something lightweight, plural                                          noun

First, my _____ shrinks, then the rest of me, and soon I'm regular old _____ again.
          another body part                                                      your name

A beam of _____ hits me, and I'm lifted into a giant _____ in the sky.
          something soft, plural                               noun

A(n) _____ piloting it orders me to _____ _____, and we
     animal                                   verb              adverb ending in -ly

take off at warp speed. I close my eyes, and when I open them I'm back in _____,
                                                                          hometown

in my _____. I'm totally _____. Was it all a dream? Then I wiggle my tail.
      type of furniture            emotion

---

## Published by the National Geographic Society

John M. Fahey, *Chairman of the Board and Chief Executive Officer*
Declan Moore, *Executive Vice President; President, Publishing and Travel*
Melina Gerosa Bellows, *Publisher and Chief Creative Officer, Books, Kids, and Family*

### Prepared by the Book Division

Hector Sierra, *Senior Vice President and General Manager*
Nancy Laties Feresten, *Senior Vice President, Kids Publishing and Media*
Jennifer Emmett, *Vice President, Editorial Director, Kids Books*
Eva Absher-Schantz, *Design Director, Kids Publishing and Media*
Jay Sumner, *Director of Photography, Kids Publishing*
R. Gary Colbert, *Production Director*
Jennifer A. Thornton, *Director of Managing Editorial*

### Staff for This Book

Kate Olesin, *Project Editor*
James Hiscott Jr., *Art Director*
Kelley Miller, *Senior Photo Editor*
Ruth Ann Thompson, *Designer*
Emily Kreiger, *Writer*
Dan Sipple, *Illustrator*
Christie Zepeda, *Freelance Photo Editor*
Ariane Szu-Tu, *Editorial Assistant*
Callie Broaddus, *Design Production Assistant*
Margaret Leist, *Photo Assistant*
Grace Hill, *Associate Managing Editor*
Joan Gossett, *Production Editor*
Lewis R. Bassford, *Production Manager*
Susan Borke, *Legal and Business Affairs*

### Production Services

Phillip L. Schlosser, *Senior Vice President*
Chris Brown, *Vice President, NG Book Manufacturing*
George Bounelis, *Senior Production Manager*
Nicole Elliott, *Director of Production*
Rachel Faulise, *Manager*
Robert L. Barr, *Manager*

The National Geographic Society is one of the world's largest nonprofit scientific and educational organizations. Founded in 1888 to "increase and diffuse geographic knowledge," the Society's mission is to inspire people to care about the planet. It reaches more than 400 million people worldwide each month through its official journal, *National Geographic,* and other magazines; National Geographic Channel; television documentaries; music; radio; films; books; DVDs; maps; exhibitions; live events; school publishing programs; interactive media; and merchandise. National Geographic has funded more than 10,000 scientific research, conservation, and exploration projects and supports an education program promoting geographic literacy.

For more information, please visit www.nationalgeographic.com, call 1-800-NGS LINE (647-5463), or write to the following address:

National Geographic Society, 1145 17th Street N.W., Washington, D.C. 20036-4688 U.S.A.

Visit us online at www.nationalgeographic.com/books

For librarians and teachers: www.ngchildrensbooks.org

More for kids from National Geographic: kids.nationalgeographic.com

For information about special discounts for bulk purchases, please contact National Geographic Books Special Sales: ngspecsales@ngs.org

For rights or permissions inquiries, please contact National Geographic Books Subsidiary Rights: ngbookrights@ngs.org

ISBN: 978-1-4263-1481-0

Printed in Hong Kong

14/THK/1